Designed and produced by
Aladdin Books Ltd
70 Old Compton Street
London W1

Design   David West
Children's Book Design
Editorial Planning   Clark Robinson Limited
Editor   Bibby Whittaker
Researcher   Cecilia Weston-Baker
Illustrated by   Ron Hayward Associates
            and Aziz A. Khan

EDITORIAL PANEL
The author, Linda Gamlin,
has degrees in Biochemistry
and Applied Biology, and
has contributed to several
encyclopedias.

The educational consultant, Peter
Thwaites, is Head of Geography at
Windlesham House School in
Sussex.

The editorial consultant, John Clark,
has contributed to many
information and reference books.

*First published in the
United States in 1988 by*
Gloucester Press
387 Park Avenue South
New York, NY 10016

ISBN 0-531-17117-5

Library of Congress Catalog
Card Number: 88-50507

Printed in Belgium

THE HUMAN BODY

LINDA GAMLIN

GLOUCESTER PRESS
New York · London · Toronto · Sydney

CONTENTS

The first part of the book describes the different parts of the body: the "nuts and bolts" of which we are made. The second section explains how the separate parts of the body work together, using nerves and hormones to communicate. The third section follows the body from birth to old age, and shows how babies are born. The final part deals with health and illness. Doctors see our bodies in terms of separate systems, each with a different job to do. The chart on page 34 shows some of the most important of these systems.

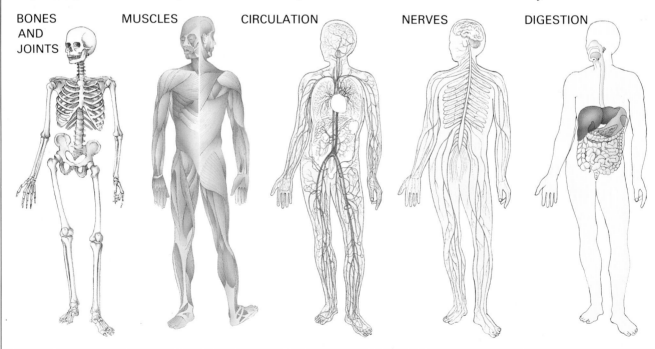

BONES AND JOINTS   MUSCLES   CIRCULATION   NERVES   DIGESTION

The front cover photograph shows a sequence of body movement.

INTRODUCTION

This book is about the human body, how it works and some of the things that can go wrong with it when we become ill. Like all living things, our bodies are made up of tiny units called cells. These are rather like the little bags of juice that make up an orange, except that they are much, much smaller. They contain a thick liquid called cytoplasm. A thin skin, known as a membrane, keeps the liquid in.

Different types of cells are found in different parts of the body, doing different sorts of work. The cells are grouped together with others of their own type, and such groups are known as tissues. For this reason, doctors talk about muscle tissue, which is made up of muscle cells, and brain tissue, which is made up of nerve cells. Another word that doctors often use is "organ" – this refers to a clearly defined part of the body that has a particular job to do. The heart, which pumps blood around the body, is an example of an organ. The brain, liver and lungs are also organs. The pages that follow describe what these organs do and how they work.

Athletic sports like hurdling test the human body to its limits.

FLESH AND BONES

The human body is 70 per cent water. Nobody is sure exactly how many cells it contains, but estimates put the number at about 100 trillion. Some cells live for only a few days and are quickly replaced, others have to last a lifetime.

Our bodies are made up of various organs, all working together in a very complicated way. It is easier to understand if we think of the body in terms of many separate systems. The digestive system, for example, processes food, the respiratory system supplies us with oxygen, and the circulatory system carries blood around the body. To get rid of waste substances, we have a urinary system, consisting, in part, of the kidneys (which filter the blood to produce urine) and the bladder (which stores urine). As part of our defense against disease we have the lymphatic system, a network of vessels which carry immune cells and link with the circulatory system. Coordinating the efforts of all these different body parts is the nervous system, which consists of the nerves and the brain, and the endocrine system, which produces hormones.

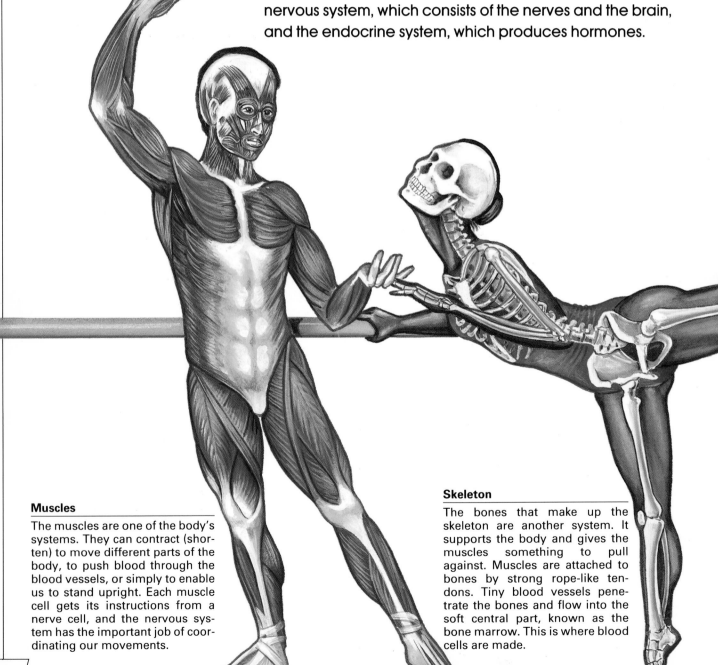

Muscles

The muscles are one of the body's systems. They can contract (shorten) to move different parts of the body, to push blood through the blood vessels, or simply to enable us to stand upright. Each muscle cell gets its instructions from a nerve cell, and the nervous system has the important job of coordinating our movements.

Skeleton

The bones that make up the skeleton are another system. It supports the body and gives the muscles something to pull against. Muscles are attached to bones by strong rope-like tendons. Tiny blood vessels penetrate the bones and flow into the soft central part, known as the bone marrow. This is where blood cells are made.

The skin

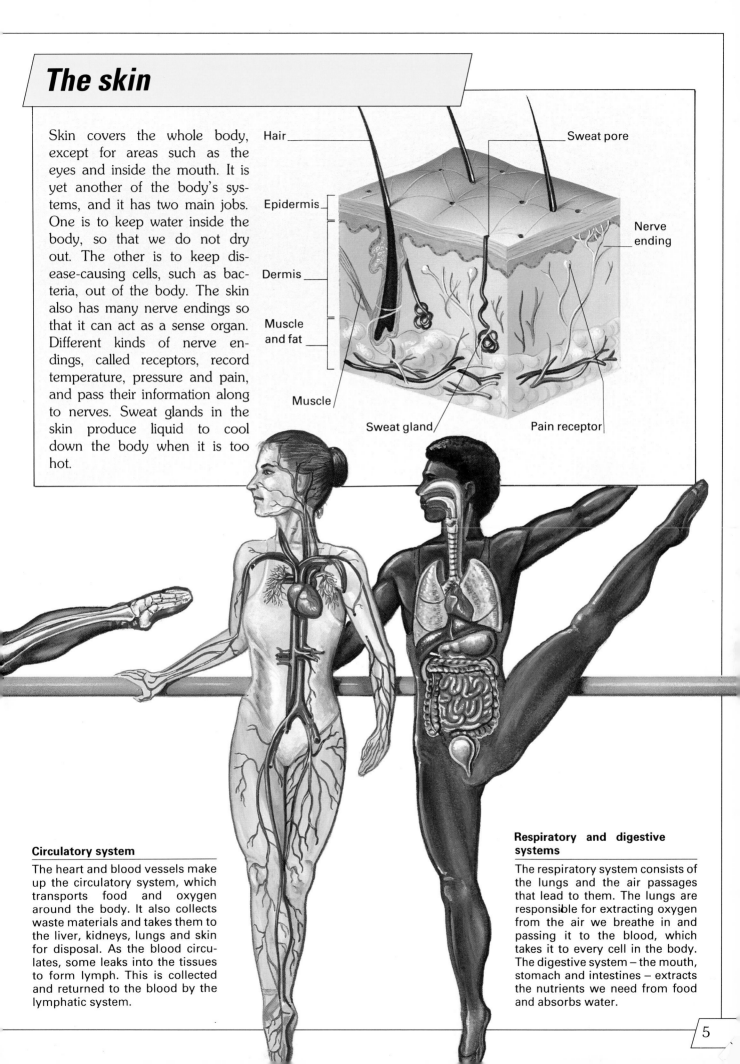

Skin covers the whole body, except for areas such as the eyes and inside the mouth. It is yet another of the body's systems, and it has two main jobs. One is to keep water inside the body, so that we do not dry out. The other is to keep disease-causing cells, such as bacteria, out of the body. The skin also has many nerve endings so that it can act as a sense organ. Different kinds of nerve endings, called receptors, record temperature, pressure and pain, and pass their information along to nerves. Sweat glands in the skin produce liquid to cool down the body when it is too hot.

Hair

Epidermis

Dermis

Muscle and fat

Muscle

Sweat gland

Sweat pore

Nerve ending

Pain receptor

Circulatory system

The heart and blood vessels make up the circulatory system, which transports food and oxygen around the body. It also collects waste materials and takes them to the liver, kidneys, lungs and skin for disposal. As the blood circulates, some leaks into the tissues to form lymph. This is collected and returned to the blood by the lymphatic system.

Respiratory and digestive systems

The respiratory system consists of the lungs and the air passages that lead to them. The lungs are responsible for extracting oxygen from the air we breathe in and passing it to the blood, which takes it to every cell in the body. The digestive system – the mouth, stomach and intestines – extracts the nutrients we need from food and absorbs water.

Almost half the weight of a normal person's body is made up of muscle. There are nearly 700 different skeletal muscles in the human body. There are also the smooth muscles in internal organs and the heart muscle. We have a total of about 50 million muscle cells.

Muscles are not used just for walking, running and lifting. They also make food move through the digestive system, make the heart beat, and help us to breathe. Some specialized muscles merely maintain our posture – without them we could not stand or sit upright. Even our skin has tiny muscles in it. They make hairs stand on end when we are cold, producing goose pimples. But muscles cannot work without energy, which comes from food. To keep us going between meals we store energy in the form of fat. If more food is taken in than is used up as energy, we become overweight.

Types of muscles

There are three main types of muscles. Skeletal muscle moves us around and maintains our posture. It is also called voluntary muscle, because we decide when the muscle should contract, although we may not be aware of making these decisions when we do something as familiar as walking. Skeletal muscle is also known as striped muscle, because it looks striped when viewed under a microscope. The second major type of muscle is smooth muscle, which is specialized for long, slow contractions. This muscle is found in the walls of the stomach and intestines (where it moves food along), in the walls of blood vessels and at various other places. We cannot make a conscious decision to contract this type of muscle, and for this reason it is also known as involuntary muscle. The third type of muscle is found only in the heart. It has stripes (like voluntary muscle), but is not under conscious control.

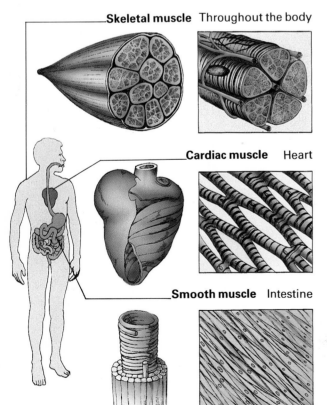

Skeletal muscle Throughout the body

Cardiac muscle Heart

Smooth muscle Intestine

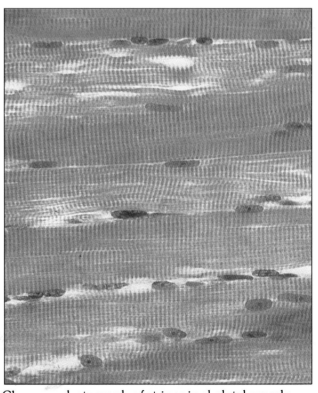

Close-up photograph of stripes in skeletal muscle

Energy and warmth

Human beings are "warm-blooded" – that is, we maintain a constant body temperature no matter how hot or cold it is. When it is cold we make our own heat by burning off some of the energy we get from food. Shivering or running can also make us warmer, because when muscles use energy to contract they waste some and the wasted energy appears as heat. (In a similar way, a bicycle pump gets hot when you use it. It is inefficient, and turns some of the energy you put into it to heat.) When we are too hot, we cool off by perspiring. The sweat evaporates, taking heat from the body.

Heat from sweating rugby players creates clouds of steam.

Muscle power

Muscles are made up of many parallel fibers, each of which is a long, single cell. Within each cell is a bundle of fibrils, and all of these contract when the muscle cell is told to do so by a nerve. Normally, we do not use all the fibers in a muscle when we make a movement. Some are kept in reserve, to be used when their neighbors get tired. During training, weightlifters increase the thickness of their muscle fibers. They also learn to contract more of the fibers at once, to give them extra strength. In an emergency, we are all capable of more muscle power than usual, because more fibers go into action. The only time that all of a muscle's fibers contract at the same time is during cramp or epileptic seizures ("fits").

A weightlifter uses all his muscles.

JOINTS AND MOVEMENT

Walking just one step involves up to 200 different muscles – almost all of the skeletal muscles below the shoulders. Our hands can make the most precise movements of all. Each contains 27 bones, 34 joints and 20 muscles.

Muscles need something solid to pull against, and most muscles work by pulling against the bones of the skeleton. The muscles are attached to bones by tendons. For example, the muscles that work the fingers are located in the forearm and reach the fingers by long tendons. Movement occurs because the bones are jointed and linked together by ligaments. These are bands of tough, elastic tissue attached to both bones. They allow the joint to move, but prevent it from being pulled too far out of position. Nerve cells tell the muscles when to contract.

Movable joints

Most joints allow movement in some directions but not in others. That is because they are a compromise between maximum flexibility and maximum strength. The hinge joint in the knee, for instance, can move backward and forward but not from side to side. The greatest range of movement is provided by ball-and-socket joints, such as those that join the arms to the shoulders and the legs to the hips. The shoulder joints are especially flexible and allow movement in a great variety of directions, something that is exploited by a good tennis player. But there is a price to pay for this flexibility, and the shoulder joint is relatively weak. It is fairly easy to dislocate – that is, to push the bones out of joint and damage the ligaments. The hip joint is much stronger, because it has to support our body weight, and so is less flexible than the shoulder joint.

Tennis uses all the movements of the shoulder joint.

Joints for movement

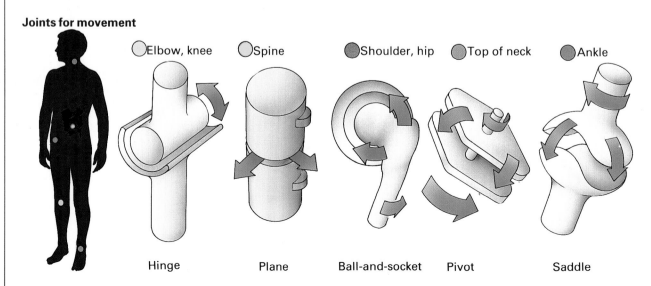

Elbow, knee Spine Shoulder, hip Top of neck Ankle

Hinge   Plane   Ball-and-socket   Pivot   Saddle

Lifting and "locking"

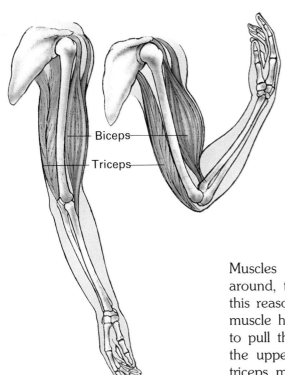

To raise the forearm, the biceps contracts and the triceps relaxes.

Biceps
Triceps

Muscles "lock" an athlete's arm joints.

Muscles cannot push bones around, they can only pull. For this reason nearly every skeletal muscle has an opposing muscle to pull the bone back again. In the upper arm, the biceps and triceps muscles form an opposing pair. The two work closely together to control arm movements. When we lift something, the bones of the lower arm are used like a lever, with the pivot at the elbow joint.

The muscles can also "lock" the elbow and knee joints. This gives the arms and legs greater than normal strength, using the combined power of the upper and lower sections of the limbs. Athletes often utilize this ability.

Oiling the joints

A car engine, or any other machine, needs oiling to keep it working smoothly. Without oil the moving parts rub together, get too hot, and eventually wear out. The same is true of the human skeleton – the joints need some sort of lubrication. But instead of oil they contain a liquid called synovial fluid. This lubrication system is more efficient than that of most machines because the synovial fluid is imprisoned in the area around the joint and cannot seep away like the oil from a machine. It is kept in place by a tough but flexible capsule, which forms a watertight seal with the bones on each side of the joint. On the inside of the capsule is a membrane, called the synovium, which holds the synovial fluid. In addition, the ends of the bones at a joint are covered with a smooth layer of cartilage, so that they glide over each other without any friction.

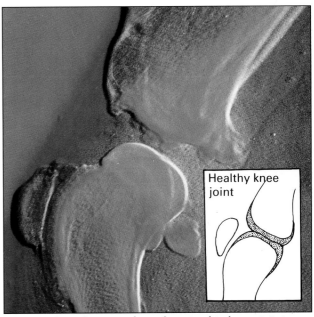

Healthy knee joint

Arthritis has destroyed cartilage in this knee joint.

Women have 4-5 liters (8-10 pints) of blood in their bodies, and men have 5-6 liters (10-12 pints). An average person has 25 trillion red blood cells carrying oxygen around the body, 50 billion white (or immune) blood cells, and 2 trillion platelets.

Most people think of the heart as the most important organ of the body, so it is surprising to discover that some small animals do not have one. A few very small creatures, such as flatworms, do not even have blood. Their bodies are so small that the things they need – oxygen and minute particles of food – can reach all parts of their bodies without any help. Humans need a circulatory system and a heart because they are so large. Without blood to carry oxygen and food to distant parts of the body, and to remove waste products, our cells would soon die.

Heart cycle

The human heart has four chambers, two to pump out blood (ventricles) and two to take it back in (atriums). There are two separate parts to the circulatory system. One carries blood to the lungs (1), where it sheds its load of carbon dioxide, collects oxygen and returns to the heart (2). The other carries blood to all parts of the body (3). During its journey around the body blood delivers oxygen (red) to all the cells, collects carbon dioxide (blue) and returns to the heart (4). It also picks up waste products from the tissues and delivers them to the liver and kidneys, which dispose of them. The blood carries sugar, fats, vitamins and other nutrients obtained from food. They are collected in blood vessels around the digestive tract. Some are delivered to cells where they are needed; others are processed first by the liver, which breaks down poisonous substances. Finally, the blood also carries hormones from one part of the body to another, so it plays an essential role in the communication between different body parts.

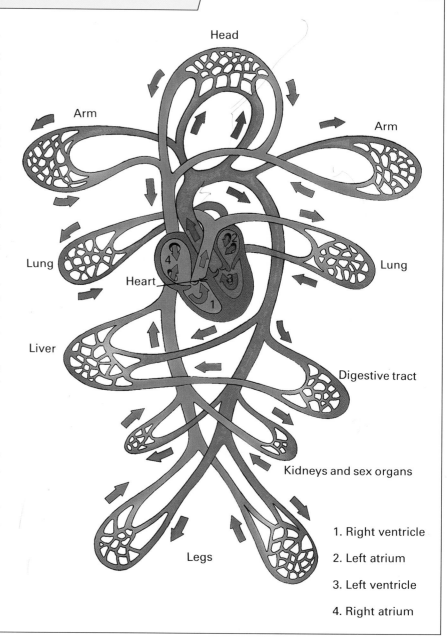

Head

Arm

Arm

Lung

Lung

Heart

Liver

Digestive tract

Kidneys and sex organs

Legs

1. Right ventricle

2. Left atrium

3. Left ventricle

4. Right atrium

Blood

Blood consists of a watery liquid containing many cells and protein molecules. These make it thick, and help it to clot if a blood vessel is cut open. There are three types of blood cells: red cells, which carry oxygen; white cells, which fight off disease; and platelets, which make blood clot around a cut or scratch. The red cells contain a red protein called hemoglobin. It binds to oxygen, which it carries from the lungs via the heart to the tissues.

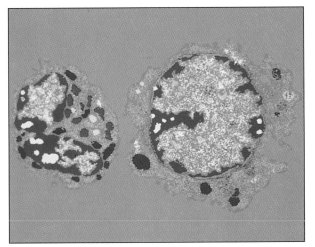

White blood cells engulf bacteria (purple) on left.

Vessels

The circulatory system is made up of a great many blood vessels. Those that carry blood away from the heart are called arteries. Those that return blood to the heart are called veins. Between the arteries and veins, the blood flows through very narrow vessels known as capillaries. The capillaries are in close contact with the cells of the body, and through them the blood can exchange substances (such as oxygen and carbon dioxide) with the cells.

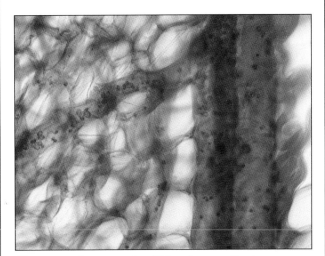

Close-up photograph of blood in capillaries

Pulse

If you put your ear to somebody's chest you can hear the heart beating. The noise is the sound the heart makes as it contracts to pump blood around the body. It is actually produced by valves in the heart as they snap open and shut to control the flow of blood. As the heart pushes blood out, it causes the arteries to expand briefly, to hold the extra blood flowing into them. If you put your fingers on an artery (such as the one in the wrist) you can feel the regular expansions as the pulse. When you are resting, your pulse should be about 70-75 beats a minute (it is faster in young children). If you exercise strenuously, your pulse rate doubles and the volume of blood pumped out with each beat also increases. The overall effect is to boost the heart's output from 5 quarts to 26 quarts a minute.

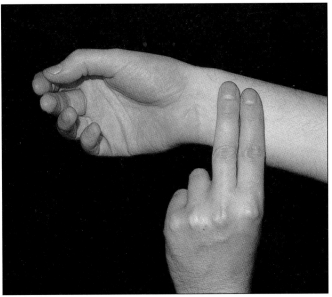

The pulse can be felt in an artery at the wrist.

LUNGS AND BREATHING

Each lung contains more than 300 million air sacs. Opened up and spread out, they would cover an area the size of a tennis court.

Air contains 21% oxygen, but the air we breathe out contains only 16% – we absorb almost a quarter of the available oxygen in air.

Lungs allow us to extract a gas called oxygen from the air we breathe. When life began on Earth, there was almost no oxygen in the air, and the earliest living things survived without it for millions of years. When oxygen began to appear, many of them died out because oxygen was poisonous to them. Humans are descended from living things that were able to make oxygen safe, and use it for their own needs. Now we are completely dependent on oxygen, but it is still dangerous to us if we take in too much – for instance, breathing excess oxygen can damage the brain.

Tubes and sacs

When we breathe in, air flows down the windpipe (trachea), through the bronchi and bronchioles and into the tiny air sacs that make up the lungs. There oxygen is extracted. It passes through the inner wall of the lung into the network of blood capillaries that surround each air sac. At the same time, carbon dioxide passes out of the blood into the lung, from which it is breathed out.

Like many gases, oxygen can dissolve in water, but it does so only if there is little oxygen already in the water. The insides of the air sacs are lined with a thin layer of watery fluid in which the oxygen dissolves. The fluid contains little oxygen at first because the blood is continually absorbing oxygen from it, with the help of the red pigment (hemoglobin) in its red cells. Hemoglobin binds to oxygen, rather as a sponge soaks up water.

To get enough oxygen, we need a very large area of fluid for it to dissolve in. The lung is divided into many millions of air sacs, to give it a much larger surface area.

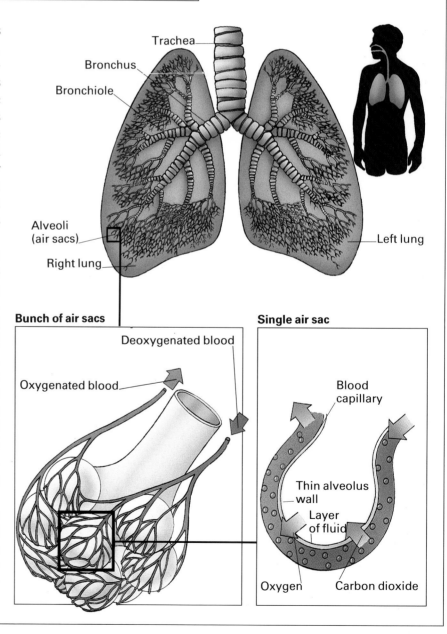

Trachea

Bronchus

Bronchiole

Alveoli (air sacs)

Right lung

Left lung

Bunch of air sacs

Deoxygenated blood

Oxygenated blood

Single air sac

Blood capillary

Thin alveolus wall

Layer of fluid

Oxygen

Carbon dioxide

Fresh air

When we breathe, we take in a lot of other things besides oxygen. Four-fifths of air is nitrogen, an inert gas we do not need and so merely breathe out again. Air also contains germs, pollen, dust and pollutants such as smoke particles, exhaust gases from cars, and gases produced by factories. The nose and lungs produce sticky mucus to capture some of the germs and particles. Also special cells, called phagocytes, wander through the lungs eating up dust, germs and other unwanted items. Tiny moving hairs, called cilia, act as a natural cleaning system, pushing mucus and dead phagocytes up out of the lungs.

Pollution from industry poisons the air we breathe.

Exchange of gases

The lungs are soft and spongy and need to be protected from damage. The rib cage not only protects them, but also helps us to breathe. Muscles between the ribs contract when we want to take a deep breath, pulling the ribs closer together and making the chest swell out. A sheet of muscle called the diaphragm also plays a part. It lies just below the lungs, and contracts when we breathe in. The only time you notice it is when you have hiccups, which are caused by sharp muscular contractions (spasms) of the diaphragm.

Breathing out is much easier then breathing in. All the muscles relax and the lungs contract of their own accord because of a very elastic tissue that surrounds them.

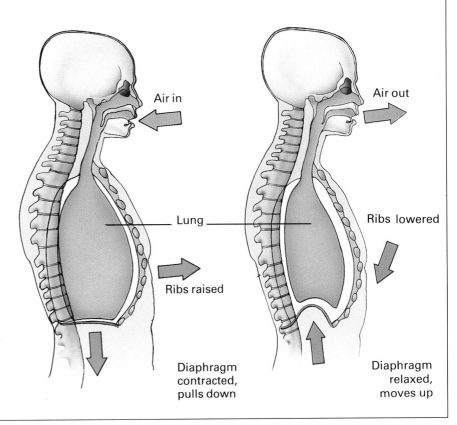

Air in

Ribs raised

Lung

Diaphragm contracted, pulls down

Air out

Ribs lowered

Diaphragm relaxed, moves up

THE DIGESTIVE SYSTEM

The digestive system would be more than 8 meters (26 feet) long if it were stretched out to its full length. The longest part, the small intestine, measures about 6 meters (nearly 20 feet). On its inner wall are about 500,000 tiny finger-like projections, known as villi. Peristalsis (see below) moves food through the body at about 2.5 cm (1 in) per minute.

Food supplies us with the energy we need to keep alive, move around, and build up our bodies. Because food comes from plants and animals, it contains many other substances in addition to those that are good to eat. The digestive system breaks down food so that the useful parts can be separated from the indigestible parts.

Plants, especially, produce poisonous toxins to try to prevent animals from eating them. We absorb toxins produced by bacteria that live normally in our intestines. The liver is the chief organ that breaks down and disposes of poisonous substances – including alcohol – that get into the body.

Where the food travels

The mouth

Food starts its journey through the digestive tract in the mouth. Chewing breaks it down, and digestive chemicals called enzymes (found in saliva) begin to attack starch molecules in the food. Saliva also makes food moist and slippery, so that it travels more easily through the digestive system. As food is swallowed, a flap of tissue, the epiglottis, closes off the entrance to the windpipe. This stops food from "going down the wrong way" – to the lungs.

The stomach

From the mouth, food travels down the esophagus, or gullet. It is pushed along the esophagus by waves of muscle contractions known as peristalsis. When food reaches the stomach, it is bombarded with a strong acid that kills bacteria and other disease-causing organisms. The acid also breaks down food, as do the digestive enzymes that the stomach produces. Muscular contractions churn up the food.

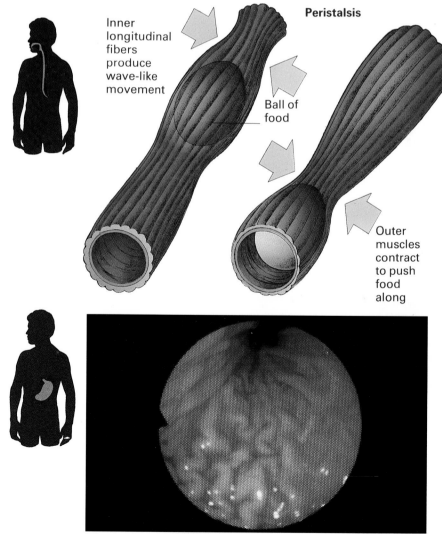

Peristalsis

Inner longitudinal fibers produce wave-like movement

Ball of food

Outer muscles contract to push food along

The folded membranes lining the stomach

The liver's functions

The diagram on page 10 shows that the blood flowing through the capillaries around the digestive system does not go straight back to the heart. It goes instead to the liver, because this is the main organ in which food is processed. The liver contains thousands of enzymes, the special substances that make biochemical reactions happen. Some enzymes break down alcohol, poisonous compounds in food, and toxins produced by bacteria in the intestines. The liver also stores iron, vitamins and glucose, the main sugar we use for energy. And it produces bile, a yellow fluid that flows into the duodenum via the gallbladder. Bile breaks up fat into small droplets that are easier for digestive enzymes to attack.

Drinking too much alcohol can cause liver cirrhosis.

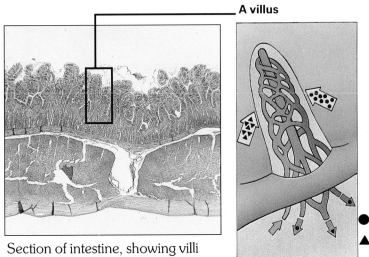

A villus

Section of intestine, showing villi

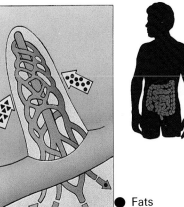

● Fats

▲ Glucose and amino acids

The intestine and liver

After the stomach comes the duodenum – the first section of the small intestine. This is where most of the digestive enzymes attack the food. Some are produced by the duodenum itself, and some by the pancreas. Bile, a liquid produced by the liver, also flows into the duodenum, to help digest fats. The remaining sections of small intestine, the jejunum and ileum, are where absorption takes place. Thousands of villi increase the surface area in these parts of the intestine, so that they can absorb food. Each villus contains capillaries in which food passes into the blood.

By the time food moves out of the small intestine, most of the good things in it (the nutrients) have been absorbed. The next stage is the large intestine (colon) which is wider but much shorter than the small intestine. Its main job is to remove water from the indigestible waste products before they leave the body.

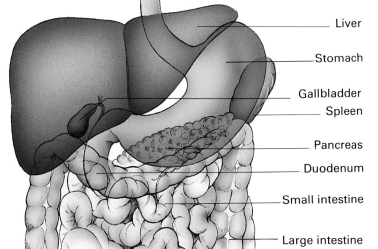

Liver

Stomach

Gallbladder

Spleen

Pancreas

Duodenum

Small intestine

Large intestine

15

COORDINATION AND CONTROL

The brain is 80 per cent water. The convoluted surface of the brain, if spread out, would cover a large television screen. The average human brain weighs 1.25 kg (2.75 lb). Some people have brains weighing almost 2 kg (4.4 lb), others only 1 kg (2.2 lb), but intelligence is not directly related to brain weight. What matters is the size of the brain in relation to the body, and the total area of its wrinkled surface.

The human body is like a complicated machine, with many different parts that must all work together. Hundreds of control mechanisms are operating inside us every second to keep the human machine running smoothly. Some of these mechanisms depend on nerves, which pass messages around the body at high speed, using electrical impulses. Other control mechanisms depend on chemical substances, known as hormones, which are slower to act than nerves but have a longer-lasting effect. These two important systems are linked in many ways. Part of the brain known as the hypothalamus receives electrical messages from other parts of the brain and translates them into chemical messages. It passes on its chemical messages to the nearby pituitary gland, which controls the release of hormones throughout the body.

Brain maps

The many nerves leading into the brain are known as sensory nerves. They bring information from the sense organs, such as the eyes, and from sensory cells in the skin. Other nerves, leading out of the brain, are called motor nerves. Most of them tell muscles when to contract or relax, although some cause hormones to be released from particular places in the body. Scientists have discovered that there are specific areas on the surface of the brain for controlling different parts of the body. There are also specific areas for receiving sensory information from each part of the body. The size of these areas indicates how important they are to us. For example, the tongue, lips and fingers are very sensitive and have large sensory areas. The hands have large motor areas, enabling the hands to make complicated movements.

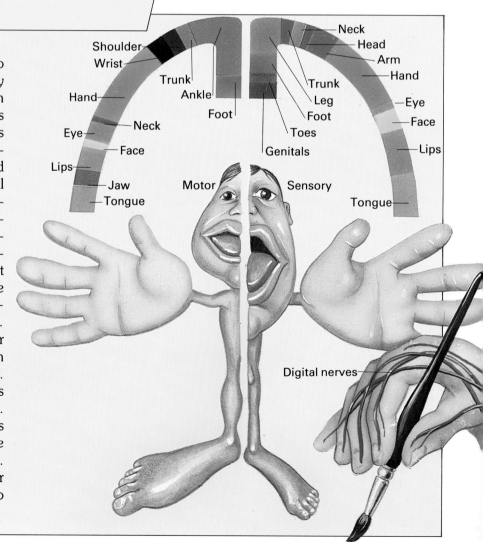

Levels of control

When we paint a picture, sensory nerves from our eyes and finger-tips feed information to the brain. The brain makes decisions about where to put the next blob of paint, and motor nerves tell the hands what to do. At the same time, our other senses remain alert – if the telephone rings, the ears tell the brain. All these reactions are under conscious control – we can decide to change the painting or to ignore the telephone. But there is another set of reactions going on all the time, which we cannot consciously control. These are directed by the autonomic nervous system, which has two separate parts. One is in charge of digestion, heartbeat, and other bodily functions. It is called the parasympathetic nervous system, and it keeps things running smoothly. The second part, the sympathetic nervous system, responds to an emergency by making the body ready for action.

Reflexes

Some reactions, called reflexes, happen automatically without involving the brain. An incoming message from a sensory nerve (purple) meets a motor nerve (orange) in the spinal cord. The motor nerve sends a message to cause the reaction. Moments later, the original message reaches the lower brain (blue), which sends signals (red) to the rest of the body.

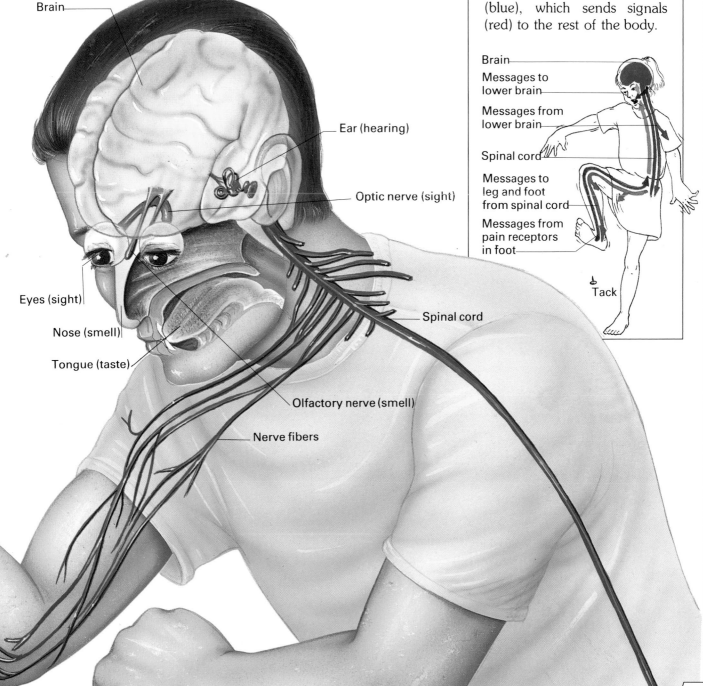

Brain

Ear (hearing)

Optic nerve (sight)

Eyes (sight)

Nose (smell)

Tongue (taste)

Olfactory nerve (smell)

Nerve fibers

Spinal cord

Brain

Messages to lower brain

Messages from lower brain

Spinal cord

Messages to leg and foot from spinal cord

Messages from pain receptors in foot

Tack

There are up to 10 billion nerve cells in the brain. Nerves can transmit messages at up to 430 km/h (270 mph). Unlike other cells in the body, brain cells are not repaired if they become damaged or die, although the function of some can gradually be taken over by others if necessary.

When you make a telephone call, a microphone turns your voice into an electrical signal, which then travels along a wire. Something very similar happens in our sense organs. They pick up outside signals, such as sound or light, and translate them into electrical impulses. The electrical impulses then travel to the brain along sensory nerves. The brain itself is nothing more than a mass of interconnected nerve cells, and our thoughts are produced by electrical impulses rushing around through the brain's nerve cells. While we sleep these impulses continue in the form of dreams.

Brain structure

The brain has many different parts, the largest being the major halves called cerebral hemispheres, in which all conscious thoughts, memory and speech processes take place. It is the outer layer (or cortex) of each hemisphere that does the work. For this reason, it is wrinkled like a walnut – to give it the maximum surface area for its size. The cerebral hemispheres are larger and more wrinkled in human beings than in almost any other animals (dolphins are our closest rivals in this respect). The hemispheres have grown so large that they cover some smaller parts of the brain that lie below them, so this diagram shows the cerebral hemispheres as though they were transparent. This reveals the small hypothalamus (which processes incoming information from the senses), the cerebellum (which coordinates the movement of the muscles) and the pituitary gland (which produces many hormones).

The brain

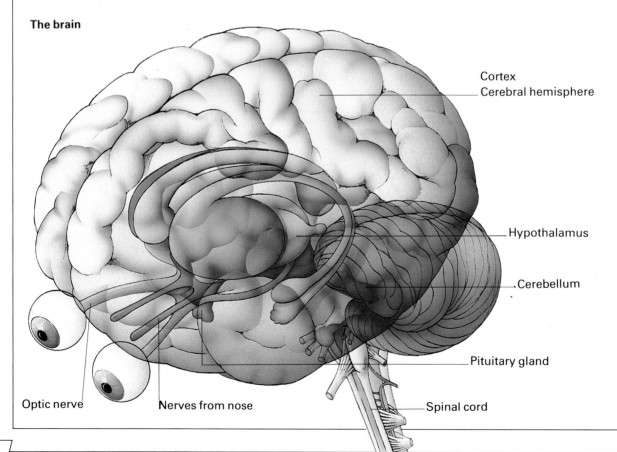

Cortex
Cerebral hemisphere

Hypothalamus

Cerebellum

Pituitary gland

Optic nerve

Nerves from nose

Spinal cord

Eyes and ears

The eye is something like a camera. It has a lens which focuses light onto a light-sensitive surface, the retina, to form an upside-down image which the brain turns the right way up. The hole in the pupil in front of the lens changes in size to allow the correct amount of light into the eye.

Sound is funneled into the ear and makes the eardrum vibrate. The vibrations travel through the three ear bones to the cochlea, which is filled with a thick fluid and contains sensory hairs. As vibrations in the fluid move the hairs, they trigger nerve impulses to the brain.

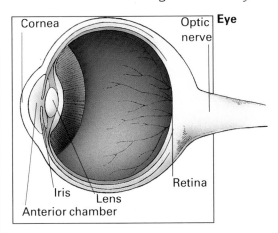

Eye

Cornea

Optic nerve

Iris

Lens

Anterior chamber

Retina

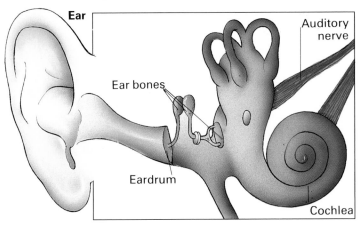

Ear

Auditory nerve

Ear bones

Eardrum

Cochlea

Nerves

Like all parts of the body, nerves are made of cells. But nerve cells are different from others because they have long extensions resembling the branches of a tree, which link with neighboring nerve cells to pass on messages as tiny electrical impulses. A nerve consists of many of these cells – perhaps running all the way from your foot to your brain – along which high speed impulses are relayed.

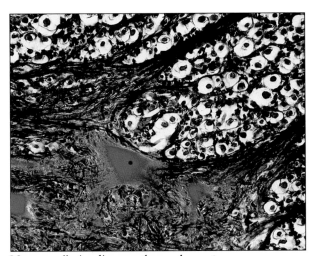

Nerve cells (red) seen through a microscope

Nose and tongue

Many people think of taste and smell as two separate senses, but they are closely linked. Both detect chemical substances. If you lose your sense of smell (perhaps because you have a cold), food seems to have less flavor because much of what you "taste" is actually the smell of food that drifts up the nose. The taste buds on the tongue recognize only basic differences– sweet, sour, bitter and salty.

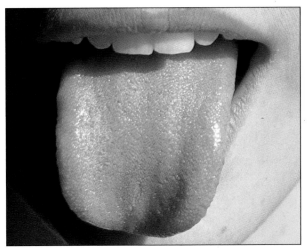

The surface of the tongue contains taste buds.

GLANDS AND HORMONES

Hormones are chemical messengers produced mainly by glands. These are known as endocrine or ductless glands because they release their secretions (hormones) directly into the bloodstream – unlike glands such as the liver or sweat glands, which release their secretions along ducts.

Nerves are useful for producing quick reactions – they are rather like the accelerator and brakes on a car. But the body also needs a control system for more gradual changes, like the gauges that tell the driver to fill up the car with gasoline or oil. This type of control is perfomed by hormones, chemical messengers that travel around the body in the blood. Hormones control growth and sexual development. They also control the levels of water, mineral salts and glucose (sugar) in the body. And hormones prepare us for action in an emergency.

How hormones work

Hormones are produced by particular areas of the body, called glands. There are two different types of hormones, ones that produce short-term, day-to-day (or even hour-to-hour) changes, and ones that produce long-term effects. The first group are nitrogen-containing substances (proteins). Well-known examples include adrenalin and insulin, which controls glucose levels and is lacking in people who suffer from diabetes. Hormones of this type do not penetrate the cells they affect. Instead they bind to receptors on the surface of the target cell (see below), and make them respond. The other group of hormones are steroids, and include growth and sex hormones. These penetrate the target cells and bind to their DNA, the genetic material. As a result, they cause long-lasting changes in the cells.

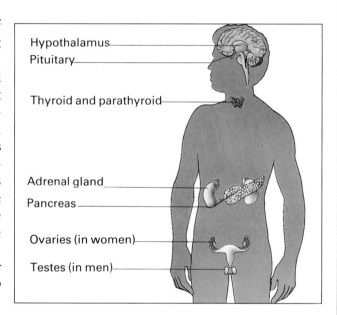

Hypothalamus
Pituitary

Thyroid and parathyroid

Adrenal gland
Pancreas

Ovaries (in women)

Testes (in men)

Hormones travel in the bloodstream to control cells

Receptor site

Hormones

Hormone binding to cell

Bloodstream

Cell responding to hormone

Flight or fight

Our ancestors lived in a world where large predators such as lions and leopards were a constant threat. They had to have a way of quickly mobilizing all their bodily resources to escape from their enemies – or fight them off. The hormones known as adrenalin and noradrenalin – the "flight or fight" hormones – are released when the brain perceives danger and have a dramatic effect on the body. They make the heart beat faster and the lungs work harder. They raise the blood pressure and boost the supply of blood to the muscles, so that they can be more active. Extra energy is needed for all this activity, so the same hormones also tell the liver to release glucose into the blood. Adrenalin and noradrenalin come from two sources. They are released from the nerve endings of the sympathetic nervous system (see page 17) and from the adrenal glands on top of the kidneys, controlled by sympathetic nerves. In the modern world, the flight or fight hormones can be bad for us – stress makes us release them far too often. They can cause damaging effects such as constant high blood pressure, which can lead to heart disease.

Fear releases "flight or fight" hormones.

Maintaining the steady state

The cells of our bodies have to have the right environment. They need to be at just the correct temperature, and to be surrounded by just the right amounts of water, salts, glucose and other vital substances. Controlling the levels of these various factors is the task of hormones.

If you go without water for a long time, special receptors in the brain detect the increase of salts in the blood. They instruct the pituitary to release antidiuretic hormone (ADH). This hormone travels in the bloodstream to the kidneys, where it instructs the kidneys to produce a more concentrated urine, containing more salts and less water. Other reactions make you feel thirsty, so that you take a drink. Similar processes occur if you eat salty nuts, or sugary cake. When this happens, hormones activate the body to reduce the amount of salt or sugar in the blood. Maintaining a constant internal environment in this way is called homeostasis.

A marathon runner gets an energy-giving drink.

REPRODUCTION AND GROWTH

A human being begins life as a fertilized egg, so small that 20 of them could fit on a pinhead. When a girl is born she already has in her ovaries all the egg cells she will ever produce – more than 200,000. By the time she reaches her teens, 95 per cent of these have disappeared, and no more than 400 ever mature. By contrast, a man produces up to 15 trillion sperm in his lifetime.

All of us start life as a single tiny cell. That cell is a fertilized egg and it is found inside the mother's body. It grows steadily in the woman's womb (uterus) until the baby is large enough to be born.

A fertilized egg cell can grow into a baby because it contains the substance DNA. This carries all the information needed to build a human body. A child gets DNA from both the parents – half from the mother and half from the father. During sexual intercourse, the father's DNA is delivered to the mother by hundreds of millions of microscopic tadpole-like cells called sperm. (Only one sperm is needed to fertilize an egg). The mother's DNA is in the eggs she produces. The moment the sperm and egg join together is known as conception or fertilization. Once it is fertilized, the egg can begin to divide to produce a baby.

Sperm and eggs

Eggs are released from the ovaries inside a woman's body. One ripe egg is released every month, normally from either one ovary or the other. It travels along a Fallopian tube to the womb. At the same time, the lining of the womb begins to thicken, in case the egg is fertilized by a sperm. If this happens, the fertilized egg begins to divide in the 5 days it takes to pass along the Fallopian tube. Once it reaches the womb, it embeds itself in the thickened lining.

If the egg is not fertilized, it passes out of the woman's body unnoticed. The thickened lining of the womb then has no purpose, so it falls away, causing a flow of blood from the vagina – the monthly period, or menstruation.

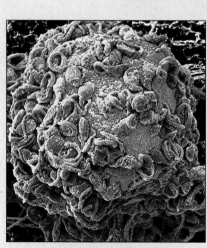

An egg surrounded by sperm

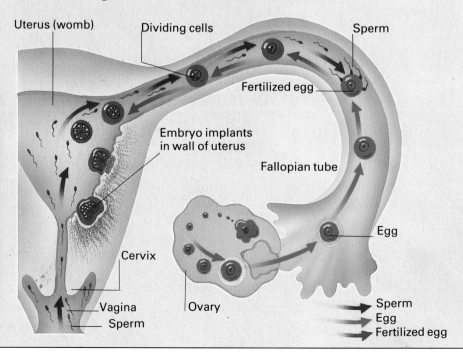

Uterus (womb)
Dividing cells
Sperm
Fertilized egg
Embryo implants in wall of uterus
Fallopian tube
Cervix
Egg
Vagina
Sperm
Ovary
Sperm
Egg
Fertilized egg

Female sex organs

The main female sex organs are the two ovaries (which produce eggs), the womb or uterus (in which a baby develops) and the vagina (which leads to the outside). The cervix is the neck of the womb, a narrow region where the vagina joins onto the womb. Fertilization – the combination of a sperm and an egg (see diagram, opposite) takes place in one of the Fallopian tubes.

Male sex organs

The main male sex organs are the testicles or testes (which produce sperm) and the penis (which puts sperm into a woman's body). The testicles are contained in the scrotal sac. Sperm move from the testicles to the penis along a tube called the vas deferens. On the way, special fluid from the seminal vesicles is added to it, to produce a white liquid called semen.

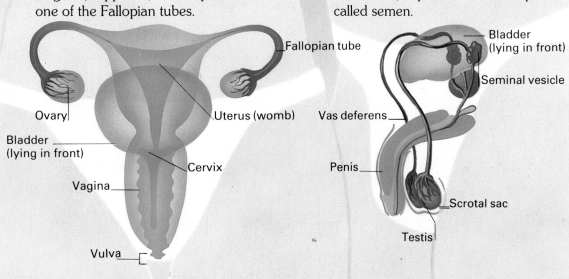

Fallopian tube

Ovary

Bladder
(lying in front)

Vagina

Vulva

Uterus (womb)

Cervix

Bladder
(lying in front)

Seminal vesicle

Vas deferens

Penis

Scrotal sac

Testis

PREGNANCY AND BIRTH

Pregnancy usually lasts about 40 weeks, although it can be as long as 43 weeks or as short as 26 weeks. An embryo begins as a single cell. After about five days it consists of 16 cells. By the time it is born, the baby is made up of billions of cells.

When a woman is pregnant, her body goes through many changes. These are controlled by hormones, some of which are produced by the placenta, an organ that exists only during pregnancy and feeds the baby in the womb. The part of the ovary from which the egg cell erupted also produces a hormone. Together the hormones adjust the body to feeding the growing baby, and prevent the ovaries from releasing any more eggs. Toward the end of pregnancy the hormones stimulate the breasts to get larger, ready to produce milk after the baby is born.

The baby in the womb

Once an egg has been fertilized it begins to divide and grow. By the age of three weeks, it is smaller than a grain of rice, and shows no signs of being human. It has no eyes or limbs yet, and looks rather like a grub. This is about the stage when a woman may realize that she is pregnant because she has missed her monthly period.

By six weeks the embryo, as it is known, has the beginnings of eyes, ears and limbs. It still looks rather grub-like, and has a short tail. Unlike most mammals, humans have no tails, although we go through a stage of having one before birth. By 12 weeks the tail has disappeared, and the arms, legs, fingers and toes are well developed.

From now on the developing baby is known as a fetus, rather than an embryo. It grows rapidly and in the last few months will settle head-downward, ready for birth. Surrounding it is a liquid known as amniotic fluid, enclosed in a strong membrane (the amnion). Just before birth the amnion breaks, and the fluid pours out.

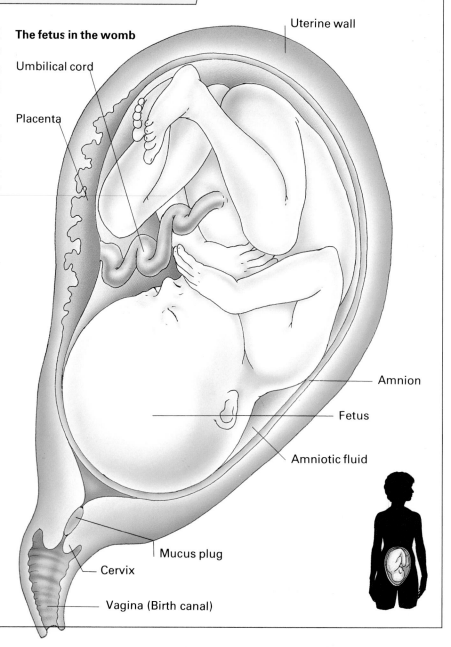

The fetus in the womb

Uterine wall

Umbilical cord

Placenta

Amnion

Fetus

Amniotic fluid

Mucus plug

Cervix

Vagina (Birth canal)

Our diet should contain enough protein to build up muscles and repair other tissues. Meat, eggs and milk are rich sources of protein, but fish and lean meat are healthier because they contain less saturated fat and cholesterol – substances that can clog arteries, even when we are young, and can later cause heart disease. Beans are also quite rich in protein, but they must be eaten together with wheat, rice or other cereals. The protein in beans complements the protein in the cereals to give a combination that is right for us. Cereals and potatoes also contain complex carbohydrate, or starch, which is a useful source of energy. So is sugar, although it can be bad for our teeth. Vegetables and fruit are rich in vitamins and minerals, and green leafy vegetables are especially important. Wholegrain cereals and vegetables also provide fiber, which helps the intestines to stay healthy.

A balanced diet is essential to good health.

Food for energy

The main source of energy in a healthy diet is complex carbohydrate (starch). Sugar is also a carbohydrate, but a much simpler one made up of smaller molecules. We do not need to eat sugar because the body can easily make energy-giving sugars, when it needs them, from complex carbohydrates or from fats and proteins. Eating too much sugar is bad for our health generally – and for our teeth.

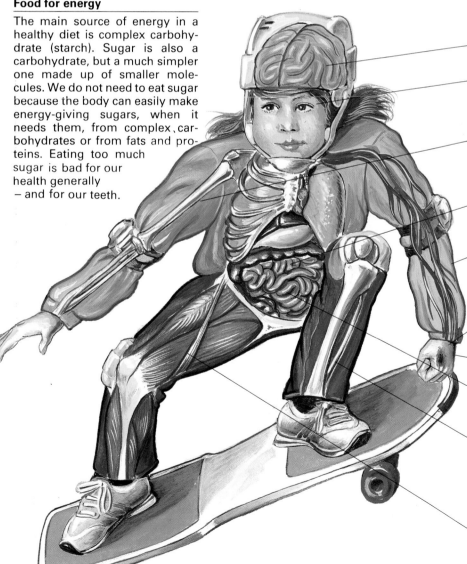

VITAMINS AND MINERALS FOR HEALTH

Vitamins B_1, B_{12} and folic acid
Brain, nerve and muscle function.

Vitamin A
For good vision, healthy skin and an efficient immune system. Toxic in excess.

Calcium
For strong bones and teeth. Calcium absorption depends on vitamin D.

Vitamins B_2 and B_5
Help to release energy from nutrients.

Iron
Part of hemoglobin (red pigment) that carries oxygen in the blood.

Vitamin C
For healthy skin and bones, and rapid healing of wounds.

Vitamin K
Helps blood to clot.

Vitamin B_6
Needed for the breakdown of protein in food. Toxic in excess.

Vitamin D
For strong, healthy bones. Toxic in excess. Not needed in the diet as long as the skin is exposed to sunlight, because the skin can make this vitamin.

Vitamin E
Protects cells from some toxic substances. Toxic itself in excess.

For every hundred body cells there is one cell with the job of defending the others against intruders. These cells which make up the immune system are produced at a rate of more than 80 million a minute, but most live for only 2-3 days.

Most infectious diseases are caused by bacteria and viruses – organisms that are too small to see but are present all around us. Defending us against these invaders are the cells of the immune system. One drop of blood contains between 200,000 and 400,000 of these cells. Some immune cells produce proteins known as antibodies, which bind to particular invaders and help to destroy them. Once the antibodies have bound to the invader, another cell, known as a phagocyte, can engulf both the invader and the antibodies. The phagocyte "swallows" the invader and kills it.

Fighting off infection

The body can make hundreds of thousands of antibodies, all of them different. If a new bacterium or virus appears, the immune system is almost sure to have an antibody that matches it. But it has only a few copies of each type of antibody, so it needs time to build up stocks of any particular antibody it needs. While it is doing this, the invader has time to multiply and spread around the body, making the person feel ill. As soon as there is enough antibody available, the immune system goes into action to fight off the invader, and the person begins to feel better.

If you have an infection, such as a cold, you can limit its spread by using a handkerchief when you sneeze and by putting your hand over your mouth when you cough. A sneeze or cough contains thousands of tiny virus particles. But with some diseases, such as measles, you may have already passed on the infection to somebody else before you realize you have it, because the virus multiplies for several days without causing any symptoms.

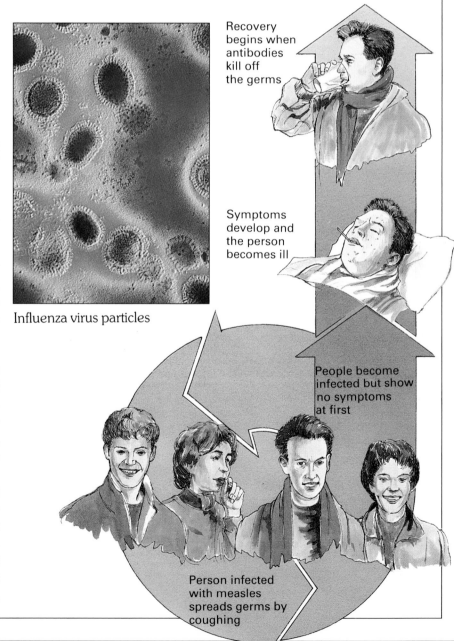

Influenza virus particles

Recovery begins when antibodies kill off the germs

Symptoms develop and the person becomes ill

People become infected but show no symptoms at first

Person infected with measles spreads germs by coughing

Vaccination

You get an infectious disease like measles only once. The first time you catch it, your body makes a type of immune cell known as a memory cell. If the memory cells for measles again encounter the measles virus, they go into action at once to produce antibodies. So the virus is defeated without you even realizing it – you are immune to measles. Doctors can create immunity artificially by vaccination. They take a small part of the virus or bacterium and inject it into you, so that your immune cells make antibodies against it. The antibodies will work against the whole virus or bacterium if it attacks you.

Vaccination prevents many infectious diseases.

 Bacterium or virus

 Vaccine

 Binding sites
Antibody

 Memory cell

| Vaccination | Antibodies appear | More antibodies plus memory cells | Memory cells remain for years | Memory cells produce antibodies |

Antibiotics

Antibiotics are drugs that kill bacteria. Doctors use them to fight off serious infections that the body cannot deal with without help. Antibiotics have saved many lives, but it is not wise to use them too freely. Some bacteria have now appeared that are resistant to antibiotics, because the drugs have been much too widely used. Such bacteria are very dangerous.

Viruses are not killed by antibiotics and there is not much doctors can do to combat them. Many viruses baffle the immune system by regularly changing their outer coat, a process called mutation. Viruses that cause colds and influenza do this, which is why people get these infections so often. Memory cells produced after the last cold do not help, because the virus has changed its coat and the old antibodies no longer fit.

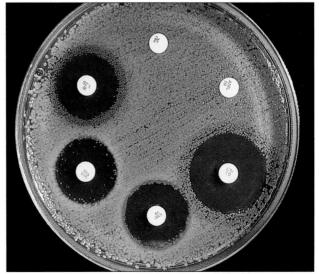
Six antibiotics under test: four have killed bacteria.

The teeth are the hardest tissue in the body. The main part of the tooth, the dentine, is 30 per cent collagen and 70 per cent mineral, just like bone. But the hard enamel coating on the outside of a tooth is 96 per cent mineral. Most adults have 32 teeth, but young children have only 20.

From looking at the fossils of early mankind, scientists know that tooth decay was rare in our earliest ancestors, who lived on meat, berries and nuts. It has only been since people began to eat sugary foods that tooth decay has become a serious problem and we have needed dentists.

Surgery, however, has a very long history. More than 4,000 years ago surgeons used stone tools to carry out the first operations on people suffering from pressure of fluid on the brain. The treatment involved cutting a hole in the skull to release the fluid. This operation is still carried out today.

Teeth

Some animals, such as sharks, produce new sets of teeth throughout their lives, so they are never without teeth, despite wear or decay. Humans are not so lucky, but they do have two sets of teeth, one during childhood (the "milk teeth") and one for adult life. The milk teeth begin to appear at about 7 months of age and have usually all emerged by the age of 2+ years. The adult teeth are waiting in the jaws, and they start to appear when the child is 6 or 7 years old, pushing the milk teeth out as they come through. These teeth have to last us for the rest of our lives, so it is very important to take care of them by not eating sugary foods, by cleaning them thoroughly and having them checked by a dentist.

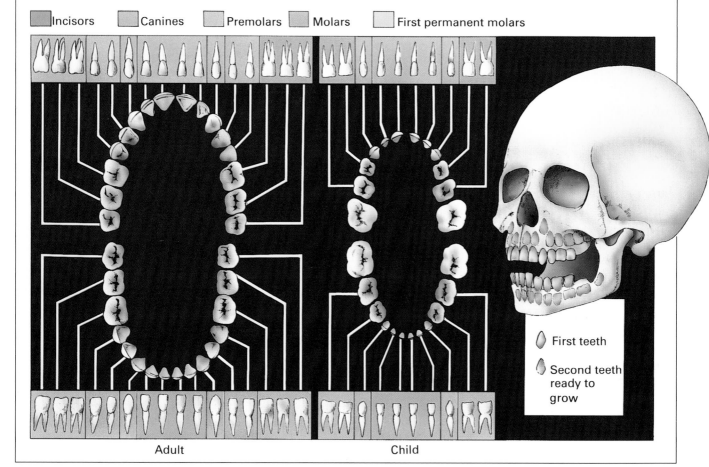

☐ Incisors   ☐ Canines   ☐ Premolars   ☐ Molars   ☐ First permanent molars

Adult

Child

◗ First teeth

◖ Second teeth ready to grow

Tooth decay

If you run your tongue over your teeth and gums a few hours after a meal, you will notice that they feel slightly rough. There is a layer of sticky material on them called plaque, and it is made up of food particles and bacteria that feed on the food. If you eat a lot of sweet things, the plaque will be even thicker because these bacteria particularly like sugar. As they break down the sugar they produce an acid which eats into the enamel of the teeth and creates cavities – the beginnings of tooth decay. There are no nerve endings in the enamel, so you cannot feel your tooth decaying until the bacteria reach the underlying pulp, when toothache really begins.

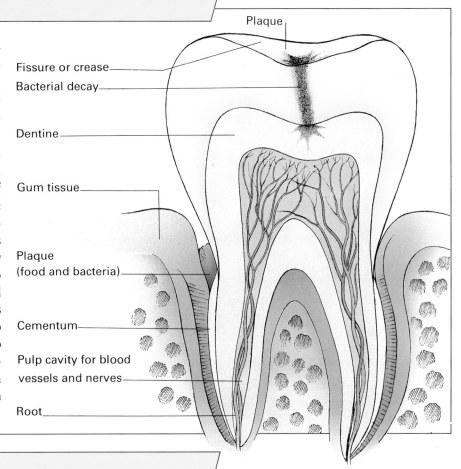

Plaque
Fissure or crease
Bacterial decay
Dentine
Gum tissue
Plaque (food and bacteria)
Cementum
Pulp cavity for blood vessels and nerves
Root

Surgery

Some disorders can be treated by taking away the part of the body that is affected and replacing it with a *spare part* from somebody else – usually a person killed in a traffic accident. Artificial *spare parts* can be used for some medical problems. The most successful are parts outside the body, such as false teeth and artificial limbs. Artificial joints made of metal or plastic are also successful, and mainly used for treating elderly people suffering from crippling joint disease. Shin plates, jaw implants and skull plates are used mostly for repairing serious injuries. A pacemaker is an electronic device that makes the heart beat regularly when the natural rhythm is lost.

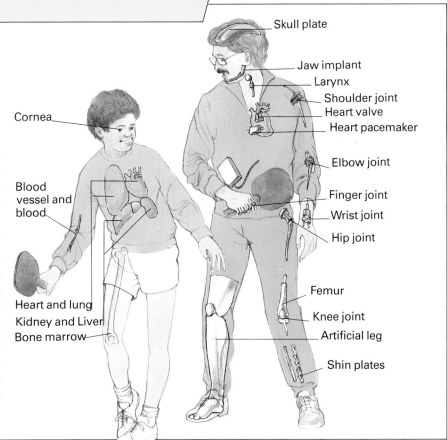

Skull plate
Jaw implant
Larynx
Shoulder joint
Heart valve
Heart pacemaker
Elbow joint
Finger joint
Wrist joint
Hip joint
Cornea
Blood vessel and blood
Heart and lung
Kidney and Liver
Bone marrow
Femur
Knee joint
Artificial leg
Shin plates

BODY SYSTEMS

The human body is made up of several systems, each consisting of various tissues and organs. The framework of the body is formed by the skeletal system – the bones and joints. Some bones surround and protect internal organs. Others, with their joints, allow movement. Power for movement comes from the muscles. The muscles and other tissues are provided with oxygen and nutrients by the blood, which is pumped around the body by the heart in the circulatory system. The action of the muscles, heart and many other organs is stimulated by the nervous system, under the control of the brain. Other nerves carry messages from the sense organs to the brain. Energy and the materials for maintaining the body come from food, after it has been processed by the digestive system.

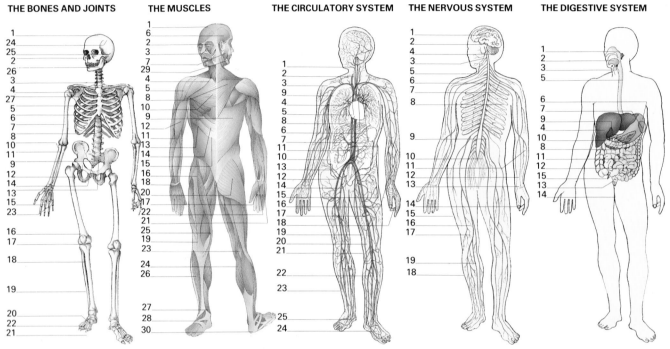

THE BONES AND JOINTS	THE MUSCLES	THE CIRCULATORY SYSTEM	THE NERVOUS SYSTEM	THE DIGESTIVE SYSTEM

THE BONES AND JOINTS	THE MUSCLES	THE CIRCULATORY SYSTEM	THE NERVOUS SYSTEM	THE DIGESTIVE SYSTEM
1 Frontal bone of skull	1 Occipitofrontalis	1 Jugular vein	1 Cerebral cortex	1 Parotid gland
2 Maxilla	2 Orbicularis oculi	2 Left carotid artery (supplying head)	2 Pons	2 Sublingual gland
3 Cervical vertebrae	3 Levator labii superior	3 Subclavian artery and vein	3 Medulla	3 Submandible gland
4 Clavicle (collarbone)	4 Sternomastoid	4 Aorta	4 Cerebellum	4 Liver
5 Sternum (breastbone)	5 Deltoid	5 Superior vena cava	5 Facial nerve	5 Esophagus
6 Rib	6 Temporalis	6 Pulmonary artery	6 Spinal cord	6 Stomach
7 Humerus	7 Masseter	7 Pulmonary vein	7 Brachial plexus	7 Spleen
8 Thoracic vertebrae	8 Trapezius	8 Heart	8 Thoracic nerves	8 Pancreas
9 Lumbar vertebrae	9 Latissimus dorsi	9 Lungs	9 Sacral plexus	9 Gallbladder
10 Radius	10 Pectoralis major	10 Liver	10 Cauda equina	10 Duodenum
11 Ulna	11 Triceps	11 Abdominal aorta	11 Ulnar nerve	11 Small intestine (ileum)
12 Pelvis	12 Biceps	12 Speen with splenic artery and vein	12 Radial nerve	12 Large intestine (colon)
13 Sacrum	13 Serratus anterior	13 Portal vein (from bowel)	13 Median nerve	13 Rectum
14 Coccyx	14 Rectus abdominis	14 Kidney with renal artery and vein	14 Digital nerves	14 Anus
15 Carpal bones	15 External oblique	15 Inferior vena cava	15 Lateral cutaneous nerve of thigh	15 Appendix
16 Femur (thighbone)	16 Abductor muscles	16 Radial artery	16 Sciatic nerve	
17 Patella (kneecap)	17 Tendons to fingers	17 Common iliac vessels	17 Common peroneal nerve	
18 Tibia (shinbone)	18 Extensor retinaculum	18 Digital arteries and veins	18 Superficial and deep peroneal nerves	
19 Fibula	19 Quadriceps	19 Femoral artery	19 Tibial nerve	
20 Tarsal bones	20 Gluteus maximus	20 Femoral vein		
21 Phalanges	21 Flexor retinaculum	21 Great saphenous vein		
22 Metatarsals	22 Muscles of wrist and fingers	22 Popliteal artery		
23 Metacarpals	23 Hamstring muscles	23 Anterior tibial artery		
24 Parietal bone	24 Gastrocnemius	24 Dorsalis pedal artery		
25 Temporal bone	25 Sartorius	25 Posterior tibial artery		
26 Mandible	26 Tibialis anticus			
27 Scapula	27 Soleus			
	28 Extensor retinaculum			
	29 Orbicularis oris			
	30 Achilles tendon			

GLOSSARY

artery blood vessel that carries blood away from the heart.

capillary very small blood vessel that carries blood between arteries and veins. Capillaries are highly branched so that they come into contact with every cell in the body. They deliver food and oxygen to the cells, and take away waste products.

carbon dioxide gas that is produced by the body when it uses oxygen. It is carried in the blood to the lungs, where it is breathed out.

cell microscopic building block of which living things are made. A cell consists of an outer membrane, surrounding a jelly-like material (cytoplasm) made up mainly of water and proteins. At its center is the nucleus, which is enclosed by its own membrane. Inside the nucleus are chromosomes, thread-like bodies that contain a cell's DNA.

DNA molecule that contains all the genetic information, which is passed from parents to offspring and tells the body how to develop. DNA is a very long molecule, consisting of two twisted strands. Each strand is made up of strings of smaller molecules called bases. There are four different bases and their order along the DNA molecule tells a cell how to make the proteins it needs. These proteins include enzymes, which control other processes within and outside cells. So by determining the types of proteins that are made, DNA controls everything else as well.

enzyme special type of protein that is very important to all living organisms. Enzymes control all the chemical reactions within our bodies. Most control one particular reaction only. For example, one causes glucose molecules to split into two parts. Another makes glucose molecules join together to make long strands (which can be stored in the liver). The digestive system has specialized enzymes that break down the molecules in food.

glucose substance that the body uses for energy. It is a type of sugar. We do not have to actually eat glucose, because the body can make it from other foods. The blood carries glucose around the body to provide energy, and the liver stores it for when we need more than we can get from food.

hormone chemical messenger that tells different parts of the body what to do. Hormones are produced by special tissues and organs known as glands.

joint point at which two bones meet. Most joints allow movement, although this is restricted to certain directions only. Some joints are fixed and do not allow movement (such as the joints between the bones of an adult's skull).

ligament band of tough tissue that holds joints together. It is made of collagen, and is both strong and flexible.

membrane very thin "skin" that surrounds all cells. Membranes are also found inside cells, where they help to organize the activities of enzymes, and keep one part of a cell separate from another. Other membranes line various organs of the body.

molecule combination of two or more atoms that forms a chemical compound. In the human body molecules vary from small simple ones such as water, to large complex ones such as proteins and DNA.

organ distinctive part of the body, such as the heart, lungs, liver, kidney, eye and brain. Organs are made up of one or more types of tissue, and each has a particular job to do (or several jobs in the case of a complex organ such as the liver).

oxygen gas that we need in order to stay alive. We breathe it in through our lungs from air (which is 21 per cent oxygen). It helps to break down food more efficiently, and without it the brain is damaged within a few minutes.

protein type of molecule that plays an important part in the body. There are many different proteins, all doing different jobs. Muscles are mostly made of protein, and it is proteins that make them contract. Collagen, the tough, rubbery material that makes up tendons, ligaments and bones, is also a protein. So is keratin, which forms skin, hair and nails. Other important proteins include enzymes, antibodies (which combat diseases), hemoglobin (which carries oxygen in the blood) and many hormones. Proteins consist of long strands of joined-up amino acids. There are twenty kinds of amino acids. By combining various ones in different sequences, the body can make thousands of different kinds of proteins.

pulse rhythmic beat of the heart as blood is pumped along an artery (such as the one on the inner surface of the wrist, just below the large muscle that controls the thumb).

system set of organs and tissues that cooperate to do a particular type of work for the body, such as the digestive system and the nervous system.

tendon strong "rope" of tissue that joins muscles to bones. It is made of collagen, a protein.

tissue mass of cells of a similar type, doing the same job. For example, muscles are made up of muscle tissue, and lungs are made of lung tissue. Connective tissue is one important type, made mainly of the strong protein collagen with cells embedded in it. It is found throughout the body, holding other parts together.

toxin chemical substance that poisons the body and makes it ill.

vein blood vessel that carries blood to the heart.

35

INDEX

All entries in bold are found in the Glossary

Photographic Credits
Cover, title page and page 27 (top and bottom): Zefa; pages 6, 9 (bottom), 11 (left and right), 14, 15 (top), 19 (left), 22, 25 (right), 30 and 31 (both) and back cover: Science Photo Library; page 7 (top): Colorsport; pages 7 (bottom), 8 and 15 (bottom): Robert Harding Library; pages 9 (top) and 21 (bottom): Leo Mason/Split Second: page 11 (bottom), 19 (right) and 21 (top): Vanessa Bailey; page 13: Rex Features; page 25 (left): Barry Lewis/ Network; page 27 (center): Sally and Richard Greenhill.